# Contents

Longman Group Limited,
Longman House, Burnt Mill, Harlow,
Essex CM20 2JE, England
and Associated Companies throughout the world.

Longman Trinidad Ltd.,
Boundary Road,
San Juan,
Trinidad

First published 1994

Produced by Longman Singapore Publishers Pte Ltd
Printed in Singapore

ISBN 0 582 237335

## Teachers' Note

### Teachers' guides

The teachers' guides which form an invaluable
part of this course can be obtained from your
local agent, or by contacting:

Sue Thompson, Longman International
Education, Longman Group Ltd.,
(address above)

Project notes are contained in the teachers'
guides.

### Pupils' book page numbers

The page numbers in the pupils' books are
colour coded according to the area of the
syllabus dealt with:

| | | |
|---|---|---|
| red | human biology |
| green | plant/animal biology |
| brown | environmental science |
| blue | physical science |
| orange | materials |

# 1 Clouds

Why does Frances think that it will rain soon?

It will rain soon!

How do you know?

There are different sorts of clouds.

cirrus

cumulus

cumulo-nimbus

stratus

nimbo stratus

Observe the clouds in the sky each day for two weeks.
Record you observations in a chart like this.

| day | cloud | weather |
|-----|-------|---------|
| 1 | | sunny |
| 2 | ═══ | sunny |
| 3 | cumulus | fair |
| 4 | cumulo-nimbus | rain |
| 5 | cumulus | fair |
| 6 | | sunny |
| 7 | nimbo stratus | rain |
| 8 | | sunny |

Can you tell what sort of weather you will have by looking at the clouds?

Do you get some sorts of clouds more often on sunny days?

Do you get some sorts of clouds more often on rainy days?

Do you get some sorts of clouds more often on fair days?

# Rain making

I wish it would stop raining

It will soon

Rain falls from clouds.
Rain clouds are darker in colour.

We do not get rain when the sky is clear.

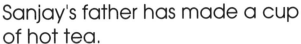

Sanjay's father has made a cup of hot tea.

Now he has to answer the telephone. He puts a saucer over his tea to keep it hot.

When he takes the saucer off, there are drops of water on it. Where do they come from?

 Write about what you have found out about rain being made.

# 3

# Air pollution

Where does dust and dirt come from?  How does it get from one place to another?  Use pieces of white tissue paper as dusters.  Wipe different places in your school.  Are some places dirtier than others?  Where do you think the dust and dirt come from?

Place four large transparent plastic strips at different sides of a building.  Put the fifth one inside the building.  Leave the five strips for a week.

Collect the five strips.  Which of the strips show traces of air pollution?  Which show the most?  Which show the least?  What could be the source of the dirt in each place?  Record your observations.  Write about how we can help to prevent air pollution in each place.  Make a poster showing ways of preventing air pollution.

# Animals on the move

When we walk or run we push against the ground.

These animals move by pushing against the ground as well.

The children are playing a game where they move like different animals.  Play a game like this.

Move like rabbits

Move like lizards

Tell your teacher how these animals 'push' themselves along. What parts of their bodies do they use to push themselves along?

| fly |
|-----|

| swim |
|------|

| slide |
|-------|

| hop |
|-----|

| climb |
|-------|

| crawl |
|-------|

| trot |
|------|

Can you match the action words to the animals and the places where they do these actions?  Draw and colour the picture and put in the animals and their action words.

# 5

## An aquarium

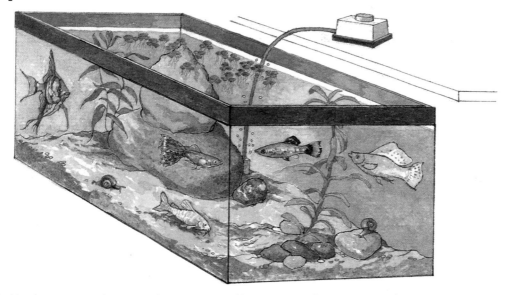

Look at the aquarium above or the one in your classroom.

Classify the things in it like this.

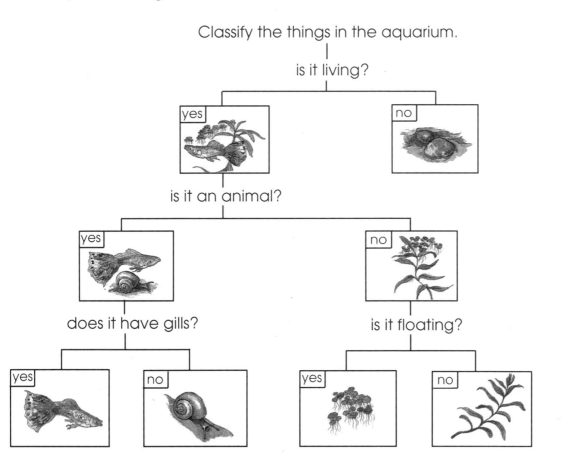

# Growing conditions of plants

Investigate what happens to plants when they do not have water.

Observe the plants every day. What do you observe? Write a report.

Investigate if plants need sunlight to grow properly. Put a box over one plant. Leave another one in sunlight.

Observe the plants every day. What do you observe? Write a report.

# The parts of a plant

Grandad has a good crop of beans.

I'll pick some for dinner

A bean seed has a baby plant and a store of food inside it, waiting to grow into a plant.

The bean plant has different parts. Find the right word label for each part of the plant.

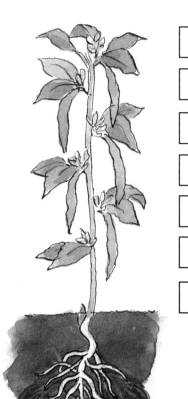

| leaf |
| --- |
| seed |
| root |
| bud |
| flower |
| fruit |
| stem |

Can you see all of these parts on the bean plant?

Find a plant. Draw it.
Show its different parts.
Name the parts and label them.
Copy the word labels above.

# Sorting seeds

Grandad grows lots of plants.
He is sorting his different seeds.
Can you sort seeds?

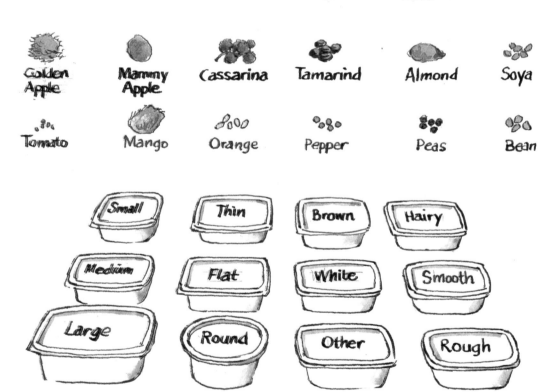

 Complete the sentences.

1   An almond seed is ____, ____, ____ and ____.

2   A mango seed is ____, ____, ____ and ____.

3   A pea seed is ____, ____, ____ and ____.

How many seeds are small?
How many are large and hairy?

Collect some seeds and describe them like this.

# Sorting leaves

Look at all these different leaves.

cucumber
hibiscus
pear
ivy
anthurium
breadfruit
maize
sugar cane
banana
coconut

You can sort leaves like this.

| long | different shades | small | hairy |

| thin in parts | dark green | medium | rough |

| round | light green | large | smooth |

A breadfruit leaf is _____ _____ _____ _____

A pear leaf is _____ _____ _____ _____

A coconut leaf is _____ _____ _____ _____

A sugar cane leaf is _____ _____ _____ _____

How many leaves are long?
How many leaves are dark green and large?
Collect some leaves and sort them like this.
Which shape is the most common? Which is the least common?

# Using leaves

We eat some leaves.
Draw and colour the favourite
leaves that you eat.

Make a list of some more edible
leaves. Which leaves do we eat
raw? Which leaves do we cook?

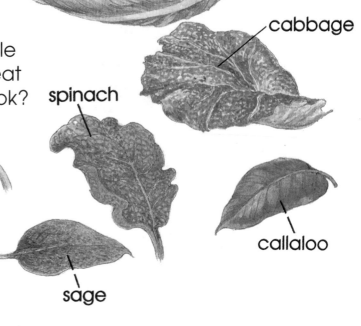

lettuce

cabbage

spinach

callaloo

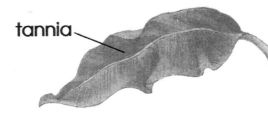

tannia

 Draw and write some short
sentences about two leaves
that we use for drinks.

sage

mint

bay

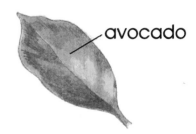

avocado

Put three leaves in order of size, smallest to
biggest. Write a sentence about each of
them.

# Herbivores

**Plant eaters** are called **herbivores**.

 Which plants do these animals eat? Copy or trace the plants and animals. Draw an arrow from the animal to the plant it eats.

Which plants do you like to eat?

# Carnivores

Here are some animals which eat other animals.

These animals eat meat. **Meat eaters** are called **carnivores**. Look closely and you will see that their eyes are on the front of their heads and quite close together. This helps them to see their prey even when it is quite far away.

Which of these animals do you think they would like to eat?

 These animals have their eyes further apart on the sides of their heads. Can you think why?

 Can you think of some more animals that eat other animals? What meat do you like to eat?

# Food chains

The plant is eaten by a caterpillar which is eaten by a bird which is eaten by a cat. This is a food chain.

The seed is eaten by a rat which is eaten by a snake. This is another food chain.

 Can you draw two or more food chains?

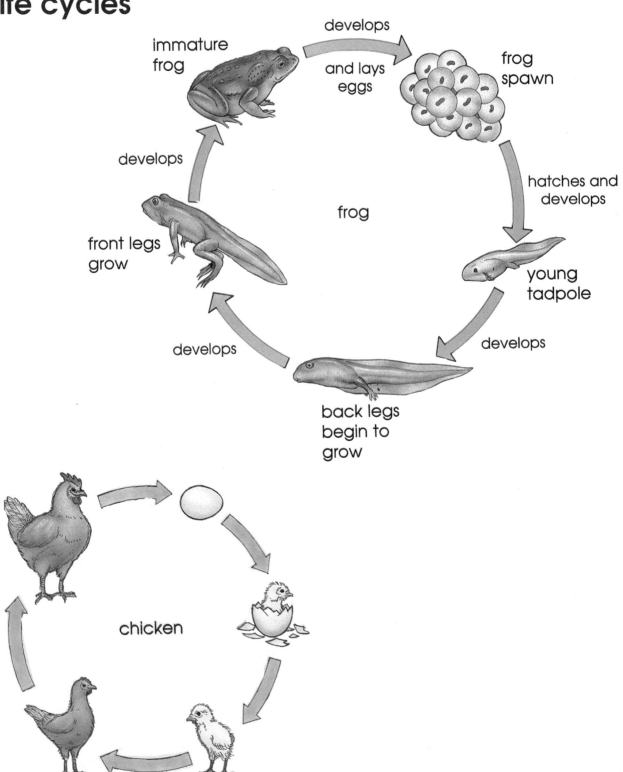

# Life cycles

develops

and lays eggs

immature frog

frog spawn

develops

hatches and develops

front legs grow

frog

young tadpole

develops

develops

back legs begin to grow

chicken

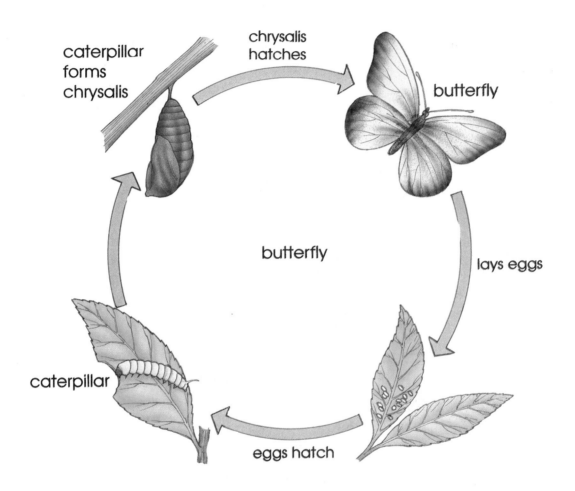

caterpillar
forms
chrysalis

chrysalis
hatches

butterfly

lays eggs

butterfly

caterpillar

eggs hatch

Look at the life cycles of these animals.
Which is the odd one out?  Why?

How is our life cycle different to all of these?
Draw the life cycle of an animal.

# Eggs

Frances found three kinds of eggs near her home.

eggs

To which animal does each belong?

Draw some animals and the eggs they lay.

Collect some frog spawn in a jar. In the classroom put it in a tank of water and observe what happens over a few weeks. Take notes and draw any changes you see.

Collect some butterfly eggs and the leaves they are on. Bring them back to the classroom and observe what happens over a few weeks.

# Growing up

Baby animals grow.
But not like this!

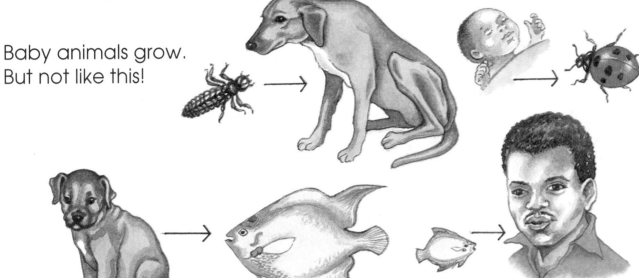

Can you sort this out?

## Measuring growth

Sanjay recorded the height of the
tallest child in each class of his
school. He drew the bar chart
opposite to show his results.

 What does his bar chart tell you?
How tall do you think the tallest child
in Class 5 will be in a year's time?

 Measure the tallest children in each
class at your school.
What did you find out?

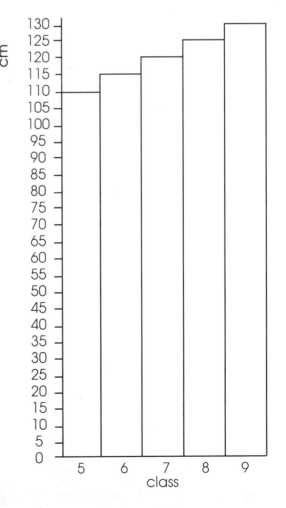

# Healthy food

Eat lots of these.

Don't eat too much of these.

 Write down what you had for breakfast.
Do you think your breakfast menu includes healthy food?

 Write down what you may have for dinner.
Does your dinner menu include healthy food?

Plan a healthy menu for a day.  Make sure it has different kinds of food, and not too much of one thing.

# Food for healthy growth

To grow properly you need to stay clean and healthy. You also need to eat different kinds of healthy foods. You should eat some of the foods from each of these groups so that you have a balanced diet.

starchy foods and fats give heat and energy

proteins and minerals from animals, nuts, peas and beans help us grow

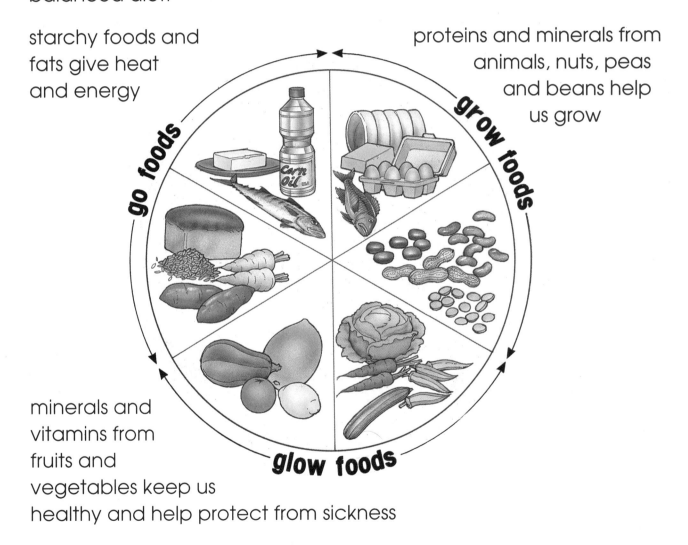

minerals and vitamins from fruits and vegetables keep us healthy and help protect from sickness

What foods do you like to eat?
Use the food chart to plan a healthy balanced breakfast.
Plan a healthy balanced dinner.

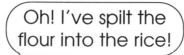

Oh! I've spilt the flour into the rice!

Will this help?

# Mixed up

Use a sieve to separate a mixture of flour and rice.
Do you know what Sanjay could do to find out how heavy the flour is and how heavy the rice is?

Weigh a mixture of rice and flour.

Separate the rice from the flour.

Weigh the rice, record its weight, then put it in a container. Do the same with the flour.

Which was the largest part of your mixture – the rice or the flour? Which was the smallest part of your mixture?
Add them both together. What do they add up to?

Separate these other mixtures. Draw a chart like the one below to record your results.

| mixture | mass | mass of heavier part | mass of lighter part | Total mass of both parts |
|---|---|---|---|---|
| Beans and rice | | | | |
| Oil and water | | | | |
| Pins and sand | | | | |

# 21

## Separating colours

Get some strips of filter paper. Measure 2 cm from the end of one of them. Make a dot with a black ink or felt tip pen. Put two more dots on top of the first dot.

Fix your strip of filter paper like this. Watch what happens. Record what you see. Try other colours. Try blue, brown, green, orange, purple, red and yellow.

water

 Copy the chart and record your findings.

| Colour | Suggest what will happen | Record what did happen |
|--------|--------------------------|------------------------|
| black  |                          |                        |
| blue   |                          |                        |
| brown  |                          |                        |
| green  |                          |                        |
| orange |                          |                        |
| red    |                          |                        |
| purple |                          |                        |

# Keeping afloat

Have you observed that some objects float and that other objects sink?

Below are some different objects. Do you think they will float or sink?

| object | I think the object will | |
|---|---|---|
| | float | sink |
| | | |

 Fill a container half full with water. Put each of the objects onto the surface of the water. Record your observations.

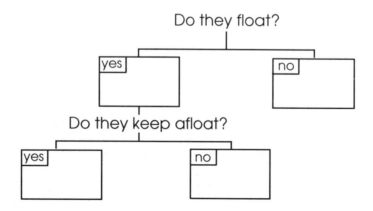

Do you know why some of them float at first and then sink?

# Plasticine boats

Sanjay thinks that heavy things sink.

A ball of plasticine is heavy and sinks very easily. Frances thinks that it will float if its shape is changed.

Can you make a piece of plasticine float?
When you have done it draw the shape that you made.

Can you make it float if you make it into a different shape?
If you can, draw another picture.

 Do all heavy objects sink? Write about what you have found out.

# Does metal sink?

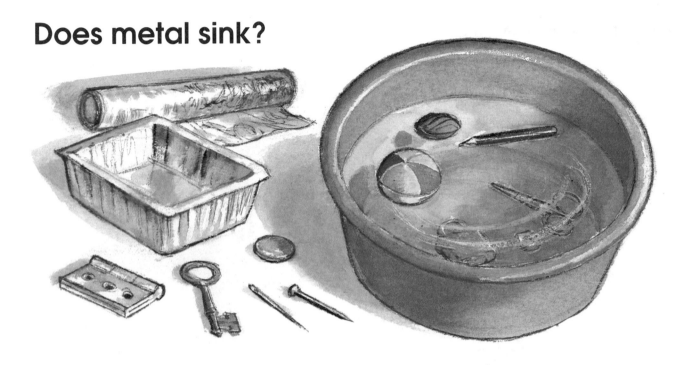

Try to float these things.  Write about what you find out.
Did the needle sink?  Sanjay shows Frances a way to make a needle float.

 Write about what you have found out.

# 25

## Using thermometers

Frances is feeling ill. The doctor is taking her temperature. He uses a **thermometer**. It measures the temperature in **degrees Celsius**.

Instead of writing the words degrees Celsius, we write °**C**. So a temperature of two degrees Celsius is written 2 °C.

Thermometers come in different shapes and sizes. They help different people to measure the temperatures of all kinds of things. What temperatures do these thermometers measure?

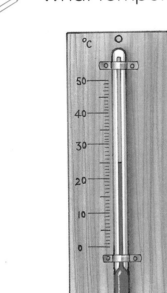   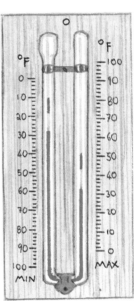

Use a thermometer to measure the temperature of warm water, cold water, your classroom and crushed ice.

Observe the teacher measure the temperature of hot water. Watch what the temperature is as the water begins to boil. This is called the boiling point of water.

The freezing point of water is harder to measure. Can you find out what it is?

# Measuring body temperature

You can use a thermometer to find out how warm
your body is.

Find out if your friends have the same body temperature as you.
Place the thermometer under your friend's arm in his or her armpit.

Leave it there for one minute.  Then take it out.

Remember to shake down the liquid before measuring the next
temperature.

 Record your measurements.

 What have you found out?

| Friend | Body temperature |
| --- | --- |
|  |  |
|  |  |
|  |  |

# Measuring and recording temperature

Sushila has observed that the temperature of the water has changed.

The water stopped boiling when we put in the frozen peas

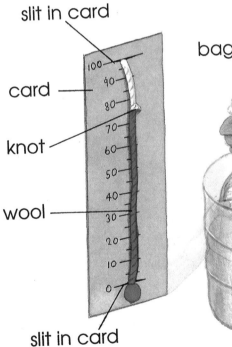

slit in card

card

knot

wool

slit in card

bag of ice

Measure the temperature of warm water in a jar. Make and use a cardboard thermometer to record the temperature.

Put a bag of ice cubes into the warm water. Observe what happens to the liquid in the thermometer.

After one minute record the temperature on a cardboard thermometer.

Measure and record what happens when a bag of warm water is placed in cold water.

Find the temperature out in the sun and in the shade. Record the temperatures on your cardboard thermometer.

# What we have learned

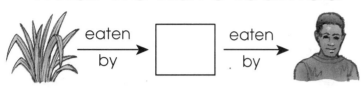

eaten by → ☐ → eaten by

**1** Which of these animals could be put in the box?
a) rat  b) lion  c) cow  d) ant

**2** Sort these into sets.

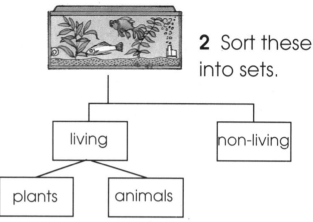

living — non-living

living → plants, animals

**3** Which of these balls could be made of styrofoam.

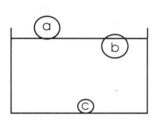

**4** What is wrong with this plant?
a)  It is in sunlight
b)  It has been watered
c)  It has air
d)  It has **not** been watered

**5** Which of these could you use to separate this mixture?
a)  magnet
b)  pencil
c)  water
d)  sieve
e)  thermometer

seeds

iron filings

**6** How are these leaves similar?
a) edges
b) shape
c) colour
d) size

**7** Which of these foods would you eat to give you energy?
a)  carrots
b)  bread
c)  oranges
d)  cabbage

**8** Draw what is missing from this life cycle.

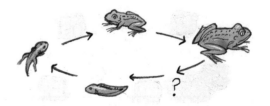

# Wind

What is making the trees move?

Is the wind always the same?

You can make a scale to show how strong the wind is. You need a bag, a rod and some marbles.

How many marbles do you have to put in the bag before it stops moving in the wind? Measure the wind in this way for the next ten days. Record on a bar graph how many marbles you need, each day.

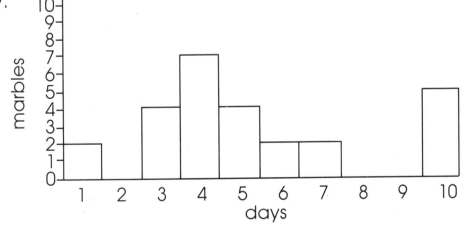

What does this bar graph tell you?
What does your own bar graph tell you?

# Rainfall

Collect rain in a test tube or a small container to record rainfall.

Look at the height of the water in the small container or test tube each day. Count the number of centimetres. Draw a bar graph to record the amount of rain you collect each day.

Remember to empty the container, after you have done your recording, ready for the next day.

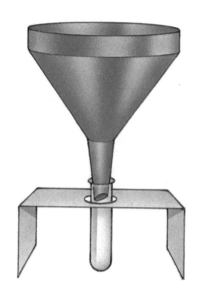

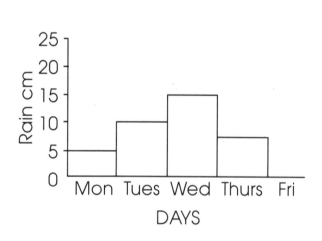

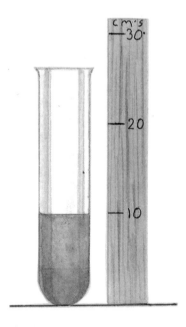

Fill in the amount of water each day for a week.
On which day did most rain fall?
On which day did least rain fall?
Did rain fall every day?
On which days was there no rain?

# Which aeroplane flies best?

Paper aeroplanes are easy to make.  Follow these instructions.

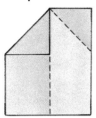 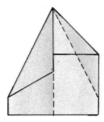 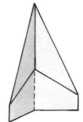 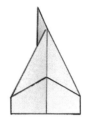 

1  Fold down centre and fold over top corner.

2  Fold corners on each side to the centre.

3  Fold down the centre.

4  Fold back a part of each half to make wings.

5  Fix paper clip to nose and a piece of tape across wings.

Fly your paper aeroplane.

You can change the design of your aeroplane by doing these things.

 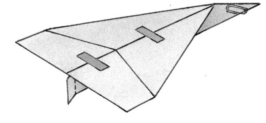

Cut tail flaps.  What happens.

Fold a rudder.  What happens?

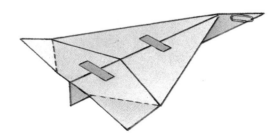

Fold wing flaps.
What happens if you fold up one wing only?  What happens if you fold down one wing only?  What happens if you fold one wing up and the other down?

Have a competition with your friends to see who can design the best aeroplane.  How will you judge which is best?  Will it be the one that flies the furthest, highest or fastest — or hits a target straight in front — or has to turn to hit a target?

 Record the results of the competition.

# Graphing plant growth

Measuring helps us to learn from our observations.

Measurements can be easier to understand if they are presented on a bar graph.

day 1 – 1cm
day 2 – 3cm
day 3 – 5cm
day 4 – 7cm
day 5 – 9cm

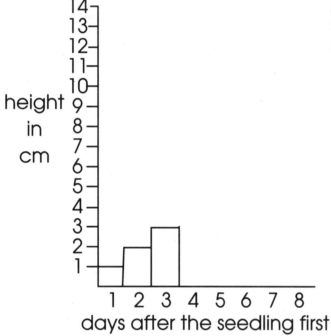

height
in
cm

days after the seedling first appears

Copy the bar graph.
Record the data for days 4 and 5.

Predict how tall the seedling will be on days 6, 7 and 8.

Plant a bean seed. Water it each day. When it appears above the soil measure it each day. Record the measurements on a data sheet.

Predict the growth for Saturday and Sunday
Measure the growth the following Monday.
Present the measurements on a bar graph.

# A trip to the beach

There are lots of things at the beach. They can be put into groups and sorted like this.

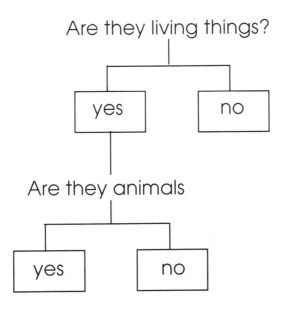

Use this chart to sort the things on the beach. Think of other questions you could ask to sort the living things into smaller groups.

# A field trip

Plan a field trip with your teacher
These things may be useful.

Look for specimens and collect some.
Record what you find.
Here are all the animals which Francis
and Sanjay observed on their field trip.

### Classifying animals

Sanjay asked some questions so that he could classify the animals.
Sort the small creatures.

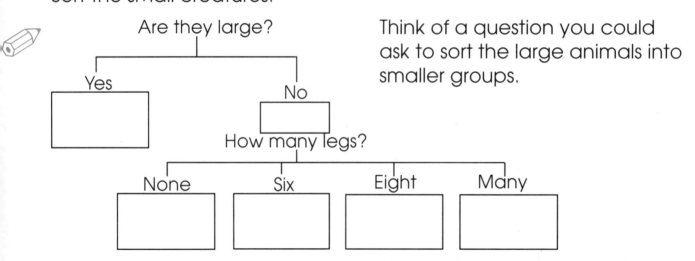

Are they large?

Yes

No

Think of a question you could
ask to sort the large animals into
smaller groups.

How many legs?

None     Six     Eight     Many

 Classify the animals which you collected on your field trip.

## A dripping tap

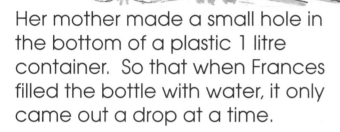

Turn the tap off properly

It's only dripping a bit

Frances investigated how much water a dripping tap wastes.

Her mother made a small hole in the bottom of a plastic 1 litre container. So that when Frances filled the bottle with water, it only came out a drop at a time.

Do the same as Frances. Put your finger over the hole. Fill the bottle with water. Take your finger off for one minute. Time this on a clock or stop watch. Record how many drops spill out in one minute. Do this 4 more times.

| Minutes | 1st | 2nd | 3rd | 4th | 5th |
|---------|-----|-----|-----|-----|-----|
| Drops   |     |     |     |     |     |

### Saving water

Water is very important to us. It is important to animals and plants. Look how this family is wasting water!

How could the people in the pictures save water?

Design a poster to make people think about being careful not to waste water.

# Measuring water loss

Frances and Sanjay investigated how much water dripped from a tap.

They recorded their measurements in a chart like this. Can you finish their chart?

How many drops will spill out in half an hour. How many in an hour?

| drops | |
|---|---|
| | 30 minutes |
| | 25 minutes |
| | 20 minutes |
| 200 | 15 minutes |
| 150 | 10 minutes |
| 100 | 5 minutes |
| 50 | |

How long did it take?

All the water has dripped out

Investigate how long it will take a dripping tap to waste one litre of water.

How much water would be wasted in a day?

Frances drew a graph to record water leaking from a pipe. Some of her measurements are missing. Can you predict how much water leaked after 4, 7 and 10 minutes?

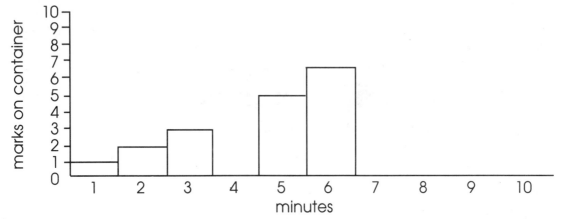

# Testing eyesight

The optician is testing Sanjay's eyes. You can test how good your eyesight is. You could use a chart like this if your teacher has one. It is called an E-Test chart. Your teacher will tell you how to use it.

Or you can make a card that is 5 cm wide by 5 cm high and draw an arrow on it. You can use it to test the eyesight of some of your friends.

Stand 40 m away from your friend. Hold the card up so that your friend can see it. Ask him or her to point in the same direction that they think the arrow is pointing. Do this five times for each friend you test.

Record your results in a table like this.

| Name | Test 1 | Test 2 | Test 3 | Test 4 | Test 5 | Total |
|------|--------|--------|--------|--------|--------|-------|
| Frances | ✓ | ✓ | ✗ | ✓ | ✗ | 3 |
|  |  |  |  |  |  |  |
|  |  |  |  |  |  |  |

Can some of your friends see better than others?

# Eyes

Your eye looks like this.
If you have a mirror you can see all of
these parts.  What colour is your iris?
What colour is your pupil?

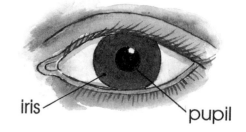

iris — pupil

 Draw an eye and label the parts.
Look closely into a friend's eye.  Look
at the pupil.  Now shine a torch into
your friend's eyes.  What happens to
the pupils?

Turn off the torch.   What happens to
the pupils?

 Write these sentences in your book
and finish them off.

**When there is less light my pupils will** _____ .

**When there is more light my pupils will** _____ .

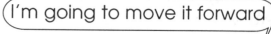
I'm going to move it forward

 Now write down why you think this
happens.

Place an object in front of a friend.  Ask
your friend to look at the object.  Look
at your friend's eyes when they do this.
Now ask your friend to step forward
and to keep looking at the same object
without moving their head.  Now move
the object to one side then the other.
What happens to your friend's eyes?

 Test more friends.  Record any changes
you saw in your friends' eyes.

# Making and using a balance

Do you know how heavy a leaf is? It is easier to measure than you think.

First you need to make a balance.

Stick two pots to a ruler.
Balance the ruler.

Put a 1 g mass in one pot. Put a leaf in the other.
Do they balance?

If not put more leaves in until they do. How many leaves balance 1 g?

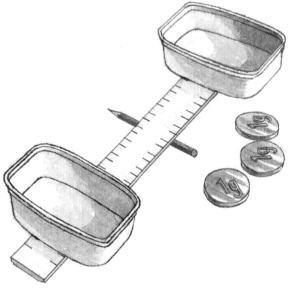

Use your balance to weigh other leaves.
Use your balance to weigh a seed.
Record your measurements.

Use your balance to measure other things and objects. Record your measurements.

# Another balance

Sanjay has another idea for making a balance to find out how heavy objects are. He uses a wire coat hanger, thin string, and jar lids.

Try to make one like this.
If you are threading your string through your lids then ask an adult to help you make the holes. You could tape the string to the lids instead.

Check that it balances properly.

Sanjay does not have enough masses so he makes some. He fills matchboxes with sand so that they balance the masses which he has.

 Use your balance to find out how heavy these objects are.

# Weak and strong forces

Forces can be weak or strong, pushes or pulls. Which of these forces are pulls and which are pushes? Which are weak and which are strong?

Fill 6 bags with sand. Blindfold someone. Put one bag of sand in one shoebox and some of the other bags in another shoebox. Tell the blindfolded person to push with one finger on each box. Ask which one was harder to push. Take off the blindfold to show the person why the box was harder to push.

Now do this again a few times. Always put one bag of sand in one of the boxes. Each time change the number of bags you put in the other box. Ask the new blindfolded person each time to say how many bags they think you have put in each box.
Record in a table like this

| Tries | How many bags were suggested? | How many bags were in the box? |
|-------|-------------------------------|--------------------------------|
| 1     |                               |                                |
| 2     |                               |                                |
| 3     |                               |                                |

What have you found out?

# Balanced forces

You can move objects by pulling them as well as pushing. Set up an investigation like the one in the picture. How many marbles does it take to move a book?

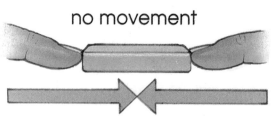

rubber band

string

carton

tray of marbles all the same size

How many marbles do you think it will take to move 2 books the same size? Try it.

How many marbles do you think it will take to move 3 books the same size? Try it.

 What about 4, then 5 books? Try it.

When the rubber does not move the forces that are acting by pushing or pulling on it are in balance.

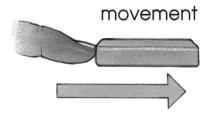

movement

no movement

These children are using forces to balance.

Try using forces to balance with a partner.

# Rubber bands and springs

Hold a rubber band like this. What makes it hang down?

You can force it down like this. What makes it stretch?

Now let go. What makes it spring back?

You could keep the rubber band stretched by hanging something on it. Which is the heaviest object? Which is the lightest object?

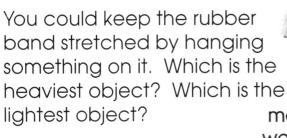

metal washer

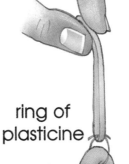

ring of plasticine

plastic washer

## A spring balance

You can use a spring to measure how heavy an object is.

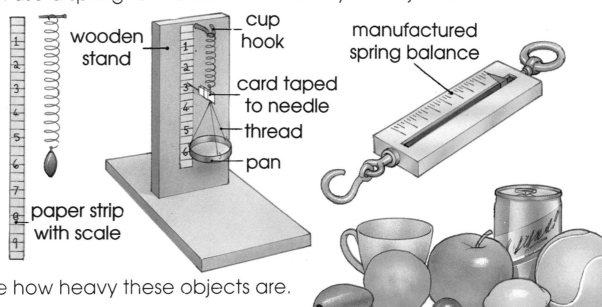

paper strip with scale

wooden stand

cup hook

card taped to needle

thread

pan

manufactured spring balance

Measure how heavy these objects are.

# Moving loads

Why is the boat on rollers?
Use a large book and some
pencils to test your ideas.
Share your results with the class.

Draw two pictures to show what
you did, one showing the book
on the desk and the other
showing what you did with the
pencils.

Write what you found out, under the two pictures.  Start your
sentences like this:

We pushed the book _____.

We used pencils _____.

What have you found out about rollers?

There are no rollers in the picture below but there are other things
which make it easier to move heavy loads.  Can you find all the
things that have wheels?  Draw two things which have wheels.

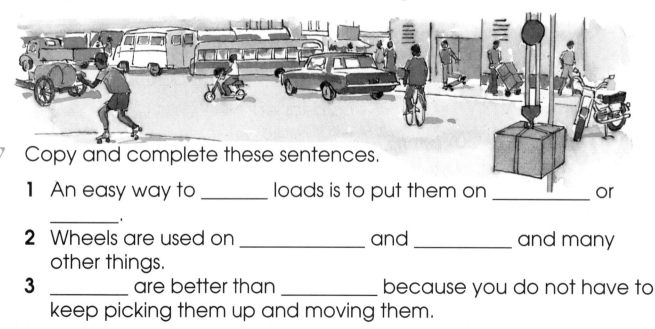

Copy and complete these sentences.

1  An easy way to _____ loads is to put them on _____ or
   _____.

2  Wheels are used on _____ and _____ and many
   other things.

3  _____ are better than _____ because you do not have to
   keep picking them up and moving them.

# 45

## Changing states of water

Water has three states.
When it is very cold it freezes.
**Frozen** water is a **solid** we call ice.
Heat some ice cubes and observe
what happens.

When ice is heated it **melts** and
changes into **liquid** water.
The freezing point of water is
___°C.

When water is heated and gets
very hot it changes to steam.
Steam is a **gas**. The boiling point of
water is ___°C.

 Write a short report of what you know about the different states of
water.

# Gases

Most gases are invisible, but there are ways of telling that a gas is present. Let us make a gas.

Pour some lime juice into a clear plastic bag. Squeeze the air out of the bag.

Then twist the middle of the bag a few times so that no air can get in it. Pour a teaspoon of baking soda in the top part of the bag. Squeeze the air out of this part as well.

Then twist the top of the bag a few times to keep air out.

Now unwind the bottom of the bag so that the baking soda can drop into the lime juice. Watch what happens.

Put your ear close to the bag and listen to what is happening. After a while squeeze the bag. What has happened?

baking powder is a solid

lime juice is a liquid

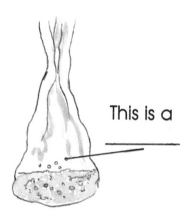

This is a

_____

# 47

## Solids, liquids and gases

Frances is making a bead necklace.  Susan is dressing her teddy.

Some solids are soft like teddy.
Some solids are hard like beads.
All solids have a shape.

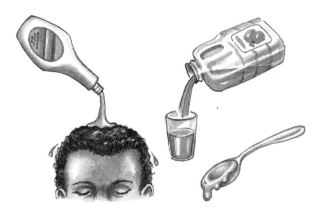

Look at the liquids in this picture.
Can you name them?
Liquids can be poured.
A liquid takes on the shape of the container it is poured into.

Look at these pictures.

Copy and fill in this table.

| Object | Solid | Liquid | Gas |
|---|---|---|---|
| fork | | | |
| bottle | | | |
| inside bottle | | | |
| balloon | | | |
| inside balloon | | | |
| bat | | | |

# Using the senses

Put some objects into different containers.

 Blindfold a friend.  See if your friend can use his or her other senses to find out what is in each container.

| Container | Suggestion | Contains |
|-----------|-----------|----------|
| 1 | | |
| 2 | | |

## Inferring by shape

Here is a game that four children can play.  You need objects of different shape, a large sheet of paper and a torch.
Do what the children are doing.

 Test one child at a time.  The child being tested must not see what objects are being used.

| Object | Suggestion | It was a . . . |
|--------|-----------|----------------|
| 1 | | |
| 2 | | |

# Having fun with shadows

Go outside in the sun. Have some fun making shadows as these children are doing. Make a shadow of a person with four arms. Draw round this on newsprint. Make some shadow shapes with your hands.

## Casting shadows

Which of these materials will make shadows?

Take the materials out into the sun. Hold them up.
Record your results in a table.

| Material | makes a dark shadow | makes a light shadow | makes no shadow |
|---|---|---|---|
| cotton | | | |
| glass | | | |
| wood | | | |

Which materials make the darkest shadow?
Which materials make the lightest shadow?

# Shadows on the move

Do you know why the shadow of the tree was in a different place in the morning? Sanjay thinks that if the position of the light source moves then the shadow will change.

Test his idea.
Stand out in the sun as early in the morning as you can. Ask your friend to draw around your shadow.

Stand in the same place two hours later and do the same thing. Then do the same another two hours later. Look at the shadows. Write two sentences about the differences.

Where do you think the shadow will be in another two hours?

I'm using chalk

I'm using a crayon

# 51

## Vibrations make sounds

A guitar makes a lovely sound
when its strings are plucked.

You can make a guitar like one of
these. It will help you to find out
how sounds are made.

Pluck the rubber band.
Watch and listen.
Write down what you see.
Write down what you hear.

Now put your rubber band around
a box which has not been cut.

Pluck the rubber band.
Watch and listen.
Write down what you see.
Write down what you hear.

Sounds are made when something
**vibrates**. A vibration is a very
quick side to side or up and down
movement. Here are some.

# Vibrations

Collect some hollow objects and
some solid objects.  Put them in
two sets.  Now tap each of the
objects with a spoon. Record in a
table like this.

|  | solid | hollow |
|---|---|---|
| good sound |  |  |
| dull sound |  |  |

Which of your objects made the best sounds?  Solid ones or hollow
ones?

Objects that have air all around
them can **vibrate** more and make
a better sound.

You can show this.
Put a few objects on a table
and tap them with a spoon.

Now hang them on a string and
tap them again.  Do they make
a better sound now?

 Record your results in a table like
this one.

| Object | Sound on table | Sound hanging up better/same/worse |
|---|---|---|
| jar | good | better |
| box | poor | same |

# Loud and soft

If you drop a can from the height of your head on a concrete path, will the sound be loud or soft?  Test your suggestion.
Was it correct?

Take 4 newspapers.  Fold them all in half.  Put them in one pile on the concrete path.  If you drop the can from the same height as before, will the sound be loud or soft?

Test your suggestion.
Was it correct?

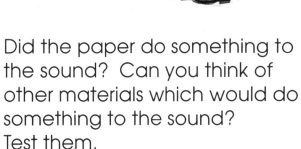

Did the paper do something to the sound?  Can you think of other materials which would do something to the sound?
Test them.

Hold the can as high as your ankle.  Let it drop onto the concrete path.  What sort of a sound do you hear?  Is it louder or softer than when you dropped it from head height.

Try making loud and soft sounds by dropping different objects from different heights.  Draw a picture of how you made the loudest sound.

# What we have learned

**1** Which of the statements about liquids is true?  A liquid

    a)  cannot be poured
    b)  is hard
    c)  takes the shape of the container
    d)  is a gas

**2** Which of these thermometers is in boiling water?

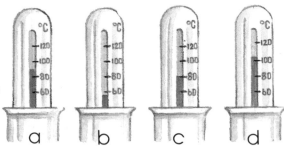

**3** This much water has dripped from the tap in one hour.

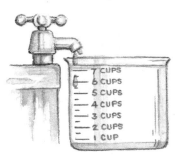

After 6 hours there will be
    a)  6 cups?
    b)  5 cups?
    c)  4 cups?
    d)  3 cups?

**4** Which part of the eye is labelled X?

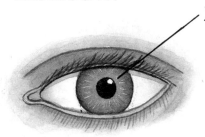

    a)  eyelash
    b)  iris
    c)  pupil
    d)  eyeball

**5** Which statement is true?
    a)  The box is heavy
    b)  The mass of the ball is less than the box
    c)  The masses of the box and ball are equal
    d)  The mass of the box is less than the ball

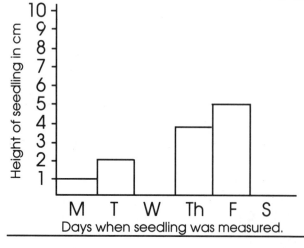

Days when seedling was measured.

**6**
a)  How many centimetres tall do you think the plant was on Wednesday?
b)  Can you predict what the height will be on Saturday?
c)  Can you predict what height it will be next Monday?